C000104523

LOOKING BACK AT
RIDDLES & IVATT LOCOMOTIVES

LOOKING BACK AT
RIDDLES & IVATT LOCOMOTIVES

The last-built Class 9F No. 92220 *Evening Star* heading the SCTS special Farewell to Steam Tour of 20 September 1964, seen here at Alton. (Strathwood Library Collection)

Kevin Derrick

AMBERLEY

First published 2016

Amberley Publishing
The Hill, Stroud
Gloucestershire, GL5 4EP

www.amberley-books.com

Copyright © Kevin Derrick, 2016

The right of Kevin Derrick to be identified as
the Author of this work has been asserted in
accordance with the Copyrights, Designs and
Patents Act 1988.

ISBN 978 1 4456 6051 6 (print)
ISBN 978 1 4456 6052 3 (ebook)

All rights reserved. No part of this book may be
reprinted or reproduced or utilised in any form
or by any electronic, mechanical or other means,
now known or hereafter invented, including
photocopying and recording, or in any information
storage or retrieval system, without the permission
in writing from the Publishers.

British Library Cataloguing in Publication Data.
A catalogue record for this book is available from
the British Library.

Typesetting by Amberley Publishing.
Printed in the UK.

Contents

Introduction

The reason for choosing to cover the designs of both of these engineers in the same book arises from their almost constant parallel career moves and the work of the elder man Henry George Ivatt preceding almost perfectly the design path of Robin Riddles and his team of engineers in the early years of British Railways. Both men began their railway lives as apprentices to the London and North Western Railway, in 1904 and 1909 respectively. As the call for men to serve their country went up for the First World War, Ivatt had become the Assistant Outdoor Machinery Superintendent at Crewe, whilst Riddles was furthering himself as a fitter at Rugby. When peace came both were laid off from the LNWR. Ivatt found himself a position as Deputy Locomotive Works and Carriage Superintendent with the much smaller North Staffordshire Railway at their Stoke headquarters. Robin Riddles managed to get himself back within the LNWR as Assistant to the Works Manager at Crewe in 1920.

As the grouping took place in 1923, work at Stoke was run down in favour of other LMS works until Stoke Works closed. Sir Henry Fowler had risen to importance within the London Midland and Scottish Railway and brought with him his loyalties to the former Midland Railway and Derby Works. Riddles remained at Crewe, whilst Ivatt secured a role as special assistant to Fowler himself at Derby. Further promotion in 1928 saw Ivatt take on the role of Works Superintendent at Derby. This brought the two men together at last, with Robin Riddles as the assistant to Henry Ivatt. Their partnership was a great success as they set about reducing the number of engines under repair from an average of 150 to just fifty at any one time. Together they supervised the construction of the second batch of Fowler's Royal Scots, considered in their time to be the most powerful in the land.

In 1931, Riddles would move on to become the Assistant Works Superintendent at Crewe at the same time as Stanier took up the reins as Chief Mechanical Engineer to the LMS. Riddles witnessed the first of the great Stanier Pacifics being built. William Stanier then went on to appoint Riddles as his Principal Assistant at Euston. Meanwhile Henry Ivatt was promoted to Electrical and Mechanical Engineer, Scotland at St Rollox Works. The paths of these two men would cross again in 1937 as they exchanged jobs.

Stanier set the standard for things to come and when No. 6220 *Coronation* set her record of 114 mph it was Riddles who was on the footplate with the crew that day, when disaster almost struck near Crewe. Before long, war broke out once more with Germany and Ivatt found himself designing a new tank for the army, while Riddles was involved in showing off *Coronation* across America. On Riddles' return to the UK, both men found themselves in the thick of projects for the war effort. Stanier was drawn into the Ministry of Production, while Charles Edward Fairburn became the CME to the LMS as all development work took a back seat to the war.

Very early in the war, the government realised that new locomotives would be required for use overseas to help with the war effort. It was Robin Riddles who took up the post which brought together the 2-8-0 and 2-10-0 designs as well as the 0-6-0ST J94 type.

In 1943, Riddles returned to the LMS while Ivatt continued as Principal Assistant, now to Fairburn, when Stanier resigned the post in 1944. Riddles was recognised for his work with a CBE in 1943 involving work on aircraft and armaments. As the war progressed it was possible to see light at the end of the tunnel again by 1944 and Ivatt began design work on locomotives. When Fairburn died suddenly in 1945, Ivatt became CME, while perhaps Riddles thought the post should be his. However, fate would take a hand once again and Robin Riddles became Vice President of the LMS and found Henry Ivatt now reporting directly to himself!

Ivatt was a credit to the post for the LMS and when Nationalisation came in 1948, it was Riddles who led a largely ex-LMS team as the new British Railways design team that was to include Messrs Bond, Pugson and Cox. Meanwhile, to aid the transition, the previous CMEs remained at their posts from the big four companies and Henry George Ivatt was the last to go in 1951, leaving Riddles in charge of the design team, as the revered post of Chief Mechanical Engineer lapsed when Ivatt left.

Kevin Derrick
Boat of Garten

Above: Perhaps a sign of what could have been if the two designers had worked together instead of in parallel. Here we see the tender from an Ivatt 4MT Mogul that may have arrived for repairs or even scrapping, which has become pushed up against Riddles Standard 5MT 73003 in the yard of Swindon Works on 8 March 1964. (Dave Down)

Released from North British during March 1945 was No. 78551, which, after service in Belgium out of Tournai once the Allies had gained a foothold in mainland Europe after D-Day, would return to Great Britain to become No. 90417 in British Railways stock. However, it would not receive the new number until September 1949. When seen on shed at Sunderland on 19 March 1967, the engine was just under six months away from its last steaming. One aspect of interest is the arrangement of bolt holes on the buffer beam to allow the fitting of a snow plough if required during the winter months. (Colin Rodgers/Strathwood Library Collection)

Staying in the north-east, we find No. 90061 sizzling nicely from the safety valves in July 1965 at West Hartlepool. The tender design was simple and robust, although unfortunately prone to becoming derailed when driven in reverse, which was not part of the design criteria for work in a war-torn Europe devoid of working turntables. (Win Wall/Strathwood Library Collection)

At the cessation of hostilities the LNER was, like the other big four railway companies, in need of additional heavy freight locomotives, and, following the example of purchasing redundant War Department Robinson 2-8-0s from many years earlier, entered into negotiations to purchase some of the now-redundant and relatively new 2-8-0s from the government to help fulfil its needs at a discount. The rival LMS of course had an affinity to its own Stanier 8F 2-8-0s, which ironically were still being built at the LNER's Darlington and Doncaster Works as late as 1946. Fourteen years later and No. 90032 was still at work on former LNER metals near March during 1960, with a healthy rake of empty sixteen-ton coal wagons. (Late Vincent Heckford/ Strathwood Library Collection)

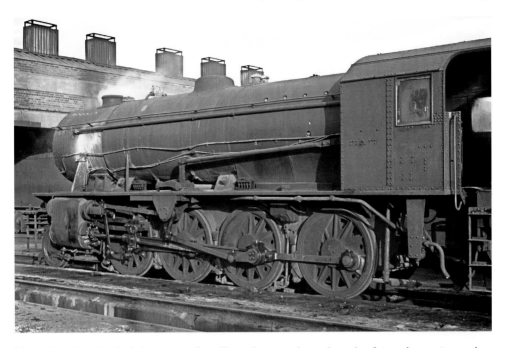

This Vulcan Foundry-built locomotive from November 1944 shows the style of riveted strapping used on some examples in the cab construction of No. 90675, in this view at New England on 6 December 1964. (Stewart Blencowe Collection)

It was as late as May 1951 when No. 90314 took up its British Railways number, and was less than thirty days away from being taken out of service when seen at Treales in late March 1965. Consigned to Cashmore's scrap yard at Great Bridge, the cutting up would be completed by August of the same year. (Chris Forrest)

Always more commonly seen on the Eastern Region handling everyday mundane but vital goods work, such as with No. 90449 near Gamston during 1961. (Trans Pennine Publishing)

With another of the Austerity 2-8-0 examples that found work on British Railways, here is No. 90602 seen close by during the same year. (Trans Pennine Publishing)

Some of the Western Region allocated 2-8-0s had their smoke-box number-plates mounted a little higher giving them a distinctive appearance, many also being fitted with brackets on the tenders for storage of fire irons along with the top feed being enclosed within a cowl. Such as No. 90573 at Taunton on 8 March 1964. (Dave Down)

As is often the case with bargain buys, by 1952 many of the class were showing signs of firebox fatigue. No surprise really as they were designed and built at a time when both man-power and materials were at an acute premium. Around one third of the class were given new fireboxes, with the work being carried out at Darlington, Crewe and Gorton. Running easily past Dukenshaw on 8 March 1961 was No. 90094. (Strathwood Library Collection)

The 2-8-0 Austerities worked on all regions at one time or another, the Southern Region losing its allocation first, with the Scottish Region having a modest allocation also, one of which was No. 90553, running tender-first at Robroyston in October 1964. The class was 733 strong on British Railways, although 935 had been built, making this the second most numerous design built in Britain. Somehow none of them survived into preservation from British Railways, considering their importance, until one was brought back from overseas in the 1970s. (Strathwood Library Collection)

The tender design was the same on the 2-10-0 version which enjoyed the larger boiler, wider firebox and a rocking grate. Conversion of these larger engines to oil-firing was much easier, although both types would run on what was often called Belgium duff, which was a low-calorific-value coal after D-Day during their war service. Under the spotlights during the Shildon 150 celebrations in 1975 was 600 Gordon, from the Longmoor Military Railway after it had closed, less than ten years before. (Aldo Delicata)

Classmate 601 was less fortunate in being used for re-railing practice at Longmoor on 3 June 1967. Introduced, like the 2-8-0 design, in 1943, just twenty-five examples from the 150 built were taken into British Railways service. All of the 2-10-0s were built by North British by 1945. (Aldo Delicata)

With such a small number in use on British Railways, and confined to Carlisle, Glasgow and Motherwell, they are seldom seen in colour. Add to this that the first pair was withdrawn in 1961 and the remainder were all withdrawn by the end of 1962, it is no wonder we had less to choose from in illustrating the class. During 1961 No. 90764 is panned by our unknown cameraman when seen at Cadder Yard running light. (Strathwood Library Collection)

Stored at Carstairs in April 1961 was No. 90768, one of twelve of the class to be scrapped at Darlington Works. The success of the 2-10-0 design, and the extra adhesion, influenced Riddles towards repeating the wheel arrangement on his 9F, rather than a compromise of a 2-8-2. More on that later. (Late Vincent Heckford/ Strathwood Library Collection)

Aside from the need to provide austerity heavy-freight engines, a need for a simple shunting locomotive was identified by the Ministry of Supply. Although based heavily on the Hunslet design, Riddles is credited with the modifications made to produce the 377 locomotives delivered from 1942 until 1945. This is one of a batch built by Hunslet as 3198/44 which became No. 68016, being ex-works at Darlington on 6 September 1959, and carrying the extended coal bunker. (Strathwood Library Collection)

Now out of use at Darlington shed on 14 June 1965 is the more common design of J94 0-6-0ST No. 68043. Although Robert Riddles first favoured the LMS Jinty 0-6-0 design, it was found that three of what became J94s could be built in the time it took to build two Jinties. In the dark days of 1942 it was a simple decision to make for the war effort. (Peter Coton)

Many of the class would be shopped at Darlington Works during their British Railways careers, with forty-seven of them being cut up at the works ultimately. One of these was No. 68025 seen alongside Darlington station whilst still in service. (Richard Icke)

Right: This one, No. 68050, would find work after 1964 with the NCB at Ashington, where she would be cut up at the workshops there instead. (Trans Pennine Collection)

Below: Along with classmate No. 68012, No. 68006 lasted into 1967, working the Cromford and High Peak line, with major servicing being carried out at Buxton where we see the well-kept engine in her last year. (Strathwood Library Collection)

Just like their bigger Austerity sisters, a number of the 0-6-0STs was retained by the army at Longmoor for training purposes. Three can be seen on a misty 16 April 1966, with WD118 carrying air brakes, which do little for the engine's looks. (Winston Cole)

The erstwhile British Railways No. 68020 which was a Bagnall-built locomotive from September 1944 found further use with the NCB at Askern Colliery after June 1963. The new keepers had fitted a ladder for access to the tanks and some strange buffers by 18 April 1970, a few weeks before she was scrapped on site. (Strathwood Library Collection)

Post-War Developments

H. G. Ivatt saw the need to introduce diesel traction after the war, with No. 10000 going into traffic for the LMS in December 1947, followed by her twin No. 10001 in 1948. This pioneer gains attention at Euston in 1960 as it departs. The 1600 hp of this design compared favourably with a Class 4 steam locomotive. Under Ivatt's auspices a single 827-hp Bo-Bo No. 10800 was ordered from North British for trials and the incredible Fell diesel mechanical No. 10100, which had an amazing sixty cylinders. Both of these locomotives were doomed for failure, although No. 10800 was noted for a few years on Rugby to Peterborough services. (Winston Cole)

Two examples of Ivatt's improved Stanier and Fowler designs are seen here at Kingmoor in March 1963, with No. 46257 *City of Salford* and No. 45535 *Sir Herbert Walker KCB*. The Patriot was one of eighteen rebuilt with improved cab, cylinders, Crewe 2A boiler, double chimney and tender, thus increasing their rating from 6P5F to 7P. Both engines were part of the 1948 programme of works. (Strathwood Library Collection)

Along with No. 46257 was No. 46256 *Sir William A. Stanier FRS* as the only two Pacifics credited to H. G. Ivatt. They were, of course, modified versions of the great man's engines, fitted with roller bearings throughout, altered rear ends and cabs, along with other smaller detail differences. The fireman on board No. 46256 checks the operation of his injectors as they pass Lancaster in 1963. (Late Ray Helm)

Other alterations to this pair were rocking grates, self-emptying ashpans, self-cleaning smoke-boxes and cab sheets. The reversers were also different to the remainder of the Duchesses. By the time of this view of No. 46257 *City of Salford* at Perth in April 1961, the original electric lighting had been removed. (Late Vincent Heckford/Strathwood Library Collection)

Towards the end of service, the cab sides of both Pacifics were adorned with the warning stripe to denote that they should not be used south of Crewe under the 25,000 V catenary. No. 46257 remained in lined green until withdrawn, whereas No. 46256 was in the (more pleasing to many enthusiasts) lined maroon livery as here at Carlisle Upperby, just days away from being taken out of service in October 1964. (Both Strathwood Library Collection)

Originally built in May 1933 was Patriot No. 45536 *Private W. Wood VC*, seen here on the curves approaching Dore and Totley in 1959. The locomotive was rebuilt into this form and released back into traffic in November 1948, to gain just fourteen years' use on the extra investment, being withdrawn in December 1962. (Trans Pennine Publishing)

Faring a little better was No. 45527 *Southport*, which managed sixteen years' use in the rebuilt condition, seen here a few months before the end in 1964. Already the crest has vanished from above the nameplate and the yellow warning stripe has appeared on the cab when photographed at Upperby. (Strathwood Library Collection)

Cast aside and withdrawn with a Jubilee at Kingmoor in early 1965 was No. 45526 *Morecambe and Heysham*. Considered almost the equal of the rebuilt Royal Scots, these rebuilt Patriots were much improved in their ride. The order to begin the rebuilding programme of the Patriots had stemmed from the successful 1942 rebuilding of the two Jubilees, No. 45735 and No. 47536, as they later became during BR, by Ivatt. (Richard Icke)

Filthy and days away from her last runs on Upperby in September 1964 was one of the pair of rebuilt Jubilees No. 45636 *Phoenix*. Unlike her namesake she would not rise again from the ashes of the cutters at Hughes Bolckows Ltd at their North Blyth scrapyard, who swiftly cut the locomotive up in January 1965. (Strathwood Library Collection)

During the time Riddles was perhaps contemplating his Standard Class 5MT 4-6-0 design, Ivatt was developing several of the later-built Stanier Black Fives. Some of the new design features would find their way into the Riddles engines a few years later. Both No. 44765, seen at Crewe and No. 44766, seen at Manchester Victoria, were fitted with double chimneys, which were found to give only marginal improvement. (Both Strathwood Library Collection)

Whereas No. 44767, seen here with Britannia No. 70031 *Byron* at Tebay in 1967, was fitted with outside Stephenson valve gear and was unique as it was normally fitted between the frames of engines. The last time it had been tried in this format was in 1884 on a GWR single-driver locomotive! (Strathwood Library Collection)

Blackpool shed was host on this day to one of twenty-two Black Fives to be fitted with Caprotti valve gear. This version is one of the plain batch built at Crewe in 1948. (Len Smith)

Ten of the Caprotti-fitted engines were given Timken roller bearings as part of the trials built alongside the others in the 1948 build at Crewe, where, along with two more classmates, No. 44751 is stored out of use at Speke Junction in January 1965. (Noel Marrison)

A more conventional-looking Black Five was No. 44675 one of eighteen Horwich-built engines from 1949 and 1950 with variations of Skefko roller bearings. She was steaming well as she left the shed at Crewe South on 5 February 1967. (Jerry Beddows)

Looking much more like Ivatt engines were Nos 44786 and 44787, the last two Black Fives built in the spring of 1951 at Horwich. No. 44787, seen here at Polmadie, combined Caprotti valve gear, Skefko roller bearings, double chimney and had the distinctive high running plate which would be featured in other designs of both Ivatt and Riddles, perhaps a little more elegantly in the case of the Standards. (Len Smith)

The New Pacifics

Originally rolled out from Crewe Works in January 1951 as the first of the 999 Standard locomotives was Britannia 7P6F No. 70000, taking the name herself, although it seems the name Great Britain was contemplated instead of Britannia. Perhaps they tossed a penny and tails won? The electrification of the WCML at Kings Langley in August 1963 suggests a short life for her breed. (Win Wall/Strathwood Library Collection)

Waiting to come off shed at 31B March in 1959 was No. 70002 *Geoffrey Chaucer*, one of six of the class named after poets. Again, the electrification of the routes from Liverpool Street, along with the arrival of English Electric Type 4 and Type 3 diesels, ousted the class away from East Anglian routes in the early sixties. (Trans Pennine Publishing)

Above and below: Fitted with the original style of handrails to the smoke deflectors is No. 70036 *Boadicea*, in the lines at Stratford on 7 June 1959. Moving around the shed the same day was No. 70013 *Oliver Cromwell*, an engine destined to be involved in the famous 15 Guinea Special of August 1968. Here already modified on its smoke deflectors to the LMR-favoured style with inset handholds. (Both photographs Late Norman Browne/Strathwood Library Collection)

Page opposite top: Passing light engine through Carlisle Citadel station we find No. 70006 *Robert Burns*, another of the first batch of twenty four of the class built in 1951. (Trans Pennine Publishing)

Page opposite bottom: Being coaled at Rose Grove on 19 March 1967 while working a special was No. 70015 *Apollo*. (Dave Livesey)

Sadly the last few years for the Britannias saw them running without nameplates and very unkempt, as here with No. 70028 *Royal Star*, making a stirring start away from Carlisle in the rain during 1967. (Strathwood Library Collection)

Again in 1967 on 14 September a nameless No. 70011 *Hotspur* at Grayrigg with a fine rake of parcels and mail vehicles in tow from Carlisle to Manchester. (John Green)

Relegation to more and more fitted goods turns in their last months finds No. 70017 *Arrow* moving easily at Farrington Junction in 1966. (Strathwood Library Collection)

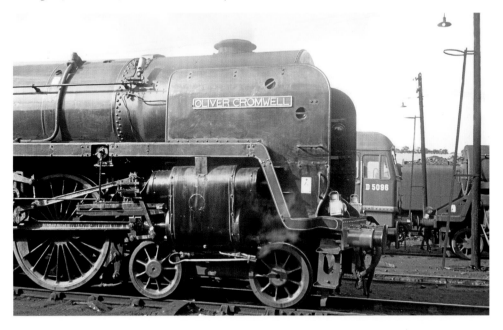

The front end of No. 70013 *Oliver Cromwell* appears to have been rough-shunted in this closer view at Carnforth in 1967. As well as the 999 Standards built by British Railways, 1,538 other steam locomotives were built to designs from the earlier companies from 1 January 1948 to the end of steam construction in 1960. (John Green)

Engaged on a Down freight working at Garsdale on 5 July 1967 was No. 70016 *Ariel*, with much steam to spare from the safety valves. (Jerry Beddows)

With a neatly painted version of the original name *Owen Glendower* was No. 70010 at Crewe South on 12 February 1967. The engine had run with the Welsh version of the name as *Owain Glyndwr* for a while the previous year. (Stewart Blencowe Collection)

Three types of tenders were drawn by the class. No. 70024 *Vulcan* at Crewe has the BR1 4250 gallon variety now in plain green livery. (Noel Marrison)

While No. 70029 *Shooting Star* was one of five of the class originally fitted with BR1A 5,000-gallon tenders, seen here topping up with water on the move at Hest Bank in 1967. (Jerry Beddows)

Ten of the class were paired originally with BR1D tenders as with No. 70050 *Firth of Clyde* ex-works at Carnforth in 1963. (Late Ray Helm)

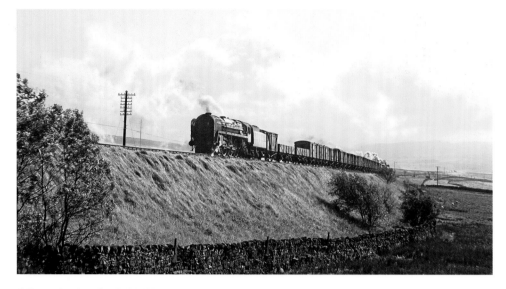

A Down freight is headed by No. 70012 *John of Gaunt* in the final fling for many of the class in late 1967, near Scout Green. (Jerry Beddows)

Enthusiasts are lineside at Preston to witness No. 70032, fitted with unofficial nameplates as *Lord Tennyson* as opposed to *Tennyson* on 3 September 1966. (Late Alan Marriott/Strathwood Library Collection)

Also built at Crewe in between batches of Britannias in 1951 and 1952 were ten Class 6P5F Clan Pacifics. Intended for routes where the heavier axle-loading of the Britannias would be a potential problem, the Clans were regarded as a disappointment which could have been filled with Standard Class 5MT 4-6-0s. Approaching Beattock in 1960 was No. 72006 *Clan Mackenzie*, one of five of the class to see use after the first five were withdrawn in December 1962. (Trans Pennine Publishing)

The profile of the smaller boiler and taller chimney of the Clans may be seen on No. 72008 *Clan Macleod* in 1966. Several of the class sported lined green cylinders towards the end of their working lives. Fifteen further Clans were to have been built, with five going to the Southern Region allocated more Anglo-Saxon names, and the other ten for Scotland continuing the Clan theme. (Len Smith)

All of the Clans were fitted with a BR1 4,250-gallon tender as fitted to forty of the Britannias. Coal capacity was 7 tons. This view shows No. 72006 *Clan Mackenzie* on shed at Dalry Road in July 1964. (Strathwood Library Collection)

Taking a break from the more regular passenger duties for the class from Glasgow to Liverpool and Manchester is No. 72004 *Clan Macdonald*, getting a goods underway from Beattock in 1960. This was one of the first of the Standards withdrawn in 1962, but with ten years' service it was not one of the shortest working Standard careers. (Trans Pennine Publishing)

Making a splendid sight at Kingmoor in 1961 was No. 72002 *Clan Campbell*. Although the Scottish Region condemned the first five of the class in December 1962, they were stored at Darlington Works for over a year, whilst consideration was given to further use elsewhere. However, it came to naught and the works cutters began their task in March 1964, with this example being the last of the five to succumb a month later. (Trans Pennine Publishing)

Mixing with other Standard types at a very smoky Polmadie in 1965 we find No. 72008 *Clan Macleod* in filthy condition, taking refuge in the shed. (Len Smith)

Although the ten Clans were well liked by their engine crews, they did show a tendency to be poor steamers when first into traffic. Perhaps intended for the very arduous Highland route to Inverness over Druimachder and Slochd summits, they settled into climbing Beattock most days, with the occasional excursion such as this one to Tyseley for No. 72008 *Clan Macleod*. Another, No. 72006 *Clan Mackenzie*, ventured down to London for a trip from Paddington to Swindon in December 1963 for another enthusiasts' special being serviced at Old Oak Common and breaking the journey at Cricklewood. It is said that Robin Riddles thought in hindsight that the Clans should have perhaps been built as a 4-8-0 design to provide a more useful and versatile engine in the power range between the Britannias and the Standard 5MT 4-6-0. It was both these and the orders being placed for diesel alternatives that put paid to the Clans so early, even though they saw trials on both Great Eastern and Midland routes. The larger and heavier Britannias were preferred if the extra power was needed over the 4-6-0s. (Len Smith)

The 1955 Modernisation Plan and large-scale orders for new diesels were on the horizon by the time No. 71000 *Duke of Gloucester* entered service in May 1954. It was the supposed gap in Class 8P Pacifics that was left after No. 46202 *Princess Anne* was destroyed in the terrible Harrow disaster and the almost complete rebuilding of No. 46242 *City of Glasgow* that resulted in Riddles seizing the opportunity to develop his own 8P design. This view of the completed engine dates from 1960 and shows it at Crewe North. (Trans Pennine Publishing)

Seen again at Crewe North in March 1963, the locomotive still carries nameplates although her tender is empty and rust is on the tyres and buffers, since being posted as withdrawn in November 1962. Seven years' service is all that this three-cylinder engine managed. The inside cylinder was driven by the leading axle and used rotary cam poppet valve gear of the British-Caprotti type. A double blastpipe and chimney, along with roller bearings to all axles, made this sole example of its type a real development of the smaller Britannia Pacifics from a few years before. (Richard Sinclair Collection)

After storage within Crewe Works, the British Transport Commission decided to retain one of the cylinders and the valve gear as an exhibit for part of the National Collection rather than the whole engine. Devoid of her tender she is seen first at Crewe Works, then in Woodhams scrapyard in early 1968. Finally, the engine was back on the long road to restoration in 1974, still at Barry. (Photos Jerry Beddows, Strathwood Library Collection and Aldo Delicata)

Standard
4-6-0s Emerge

An inspiring sight in 1961 of a lined green Class 5MT No. 73015 passing Dore and Totley when the engine was just ten years old. Sadly it would only see another five years' service. (Trans Pennine Publishing)

One of the longest-lived of this type of 4-6-0 was No. 73020, looking a little the worse for wear with steam leaks around the cylinders at Poole on 21 January 1967 in charge of a Weymouth–Bournemouth train. (Strathwood Library Collection)

Close-up of one of the Caprotti-fitted versions No. 73134 in April 1968. Originally the Class 5 Standards were to have been designed as Pacifics rather than 4-6-0s. (Jerry Beddows)

A few weeks after the previous shot of No. 73020 sees this versatile Class 5 engine engaged on a goods for Eastleigh, passing Addlestone Junction on 17 February 1967. (John Green)

130 of the class were built at Derby Works, with the remaining forty-two supplied from Doncaster. Another of the Derby engines, No. 73031, has stopped at Rotherham in 1959. (Trans Pennine Publishing)

Above: Perhaps the named engines on the Southern Region created the most interest in the Standard 5MTs, such as No. 73117 *Vivien*, passing Fleet in July 1964. (Strathwood Library Collection)

Left: Known as the Standard Arthurs, the nameplates resembled those of the Class N15s, which had previously enjoyed the same names such as, on No. 73110, *The Red Knight*. (Dave Down)

Below: Running through Weybridge in December 1966 was No. 73088 *Joyous Gard* with a pick-up goods. (John Green)

A duty much more befitting a named engine for No. 73089 *Maid of Astolat* at Basingstoke in September 1964. (Strathwood Library Collection)

Lyndhurst Road welcomes No. 73115 *King Pellinore* with the 16.10 Southampton–Bournemouth Central on 6 June 1965. Most of these named engines ran for more than half of their working lives without the nameplates being fitted as they were named after several years in service. Then, as steam started its speedy decline, many plates were removed before the locomotives were withdrawn. (Strathwood Library Collection)

A very work-stained Caprotti-fitted class member No. 73142 from December 1956 awaits a return to work at Carnforth on 30 April 1966. It would be May 1968 when the engine would have its fire dropped for the last time. (Win Wall/Strathwood Library Collection)

Another Caprotti-fitted engine to work until 1968 was No. 73133, which has come down to Eastleigh for a works repair, which will hopefully include fixing the water leak on the tender, in September 1965. (Late Norman Browne/Strathwood Library Collection)

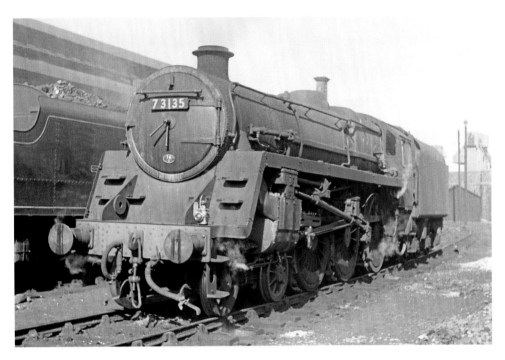

Onto Western Region territory, almost at Bristol Barrow Road for No. 73135 on 8 March 1964. Thirty of the class were built at Derby in this Caprotti form. (Dave Down)

Studies suggest that, when in good order, the Caprotti-fitted engines were almost as good as the Pacifics, indicating that the development work of Ivatt with the later builds of Black Fives was worthwhile progress. The Caprotti-fitted engines were associated most perhaps with the Scottish Region where No. 73151 is near St Rollox in September 1964. (Strathwood Library Collection)

Six tender types were carried, starting with the BR1 4,250-gallon capacity, such as No. 73002 at Westbury on 13 January 1967. (Strathwood Library Collection)

Left: At Bath Green Park shed is No. 73051, one of only three of the class paired with a BR1G 5,000-gallon tender in August 1962. (Alan Pike OBE)

Below: Doncaster Works provided a BR1B 4,250-gallon tender for No. 73171 seen at Bournemouth Central in 1964. (Trans Pennine Publishing)

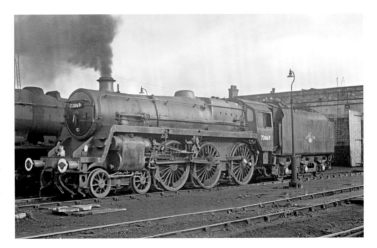

In an unlined black livery, No. 73069 is mated to a BR1C 4,725-gallon tender at Bolton on 28 October 1967. (Strathwood Library Collection)

Attached to a BR1H 4,250-gallon tender at Polmadie during June 1967 was No. 73060, just withdrawn from traffic. (Strathwood Library Collection)

Running into Basingstoke with a BR1F 5,625-gallon tender is No. 73119 *Elaine* during 1962. (Trans Pennine Publishing)

The tenders of many locomotives would be swapped from time to time, as would the regions the engines were allocated to, such as the last-built of the Class 5MTs, No. 73171, seen here near Rotherham in 1960, which ended its days on the Southern Region. (Trans Pennine Publishing)

The last active Standard 5MT would be No. 73069, catching the sun along its weathered flanks in April 1968 on shed at Bolton. (Dave Livesey)

There were no plans originally for a Class 4 4-6-0 because the thinking was that the supply of Class 5MT 4-6-0s would be sufficient. However, the Western Region was the first to ask for a lighter locomotive, perhaps in the hope that they could build more of their own Moguls. Once the Southern and Eastern Regions requested a Class 4 to replace their ageing locomotive stock, construction began at Swindon of the eighty-strong Brighton-designed locomotives. This example, No. 75033, seen at Basingstoke in 1965 was originally a London Midland Region engine. (Strathwood Library Collection)

Seen in the same year after overhaul at Derby Works was No. 75042, which would end its service career based at Carnforth when withdrawn in October 1967. (Len Smith)

In September 1962, when this picture of No. 75079 entering Weymouth was taken, the first of the class to be withdrawn, No. 75067 was still two years away from this event. However, the first example of the tank version of the Class 4 design No. 80103 was already being taken off the books. (Strathwood Library Collection)

Another of the Southern-allocated locomotives No. 75070, finds work on the 13.50 Reading–Redhill at Guildford on 27 June 1964. The later batch of engines carried double chimneys and were paired with BR1B 4,725-gallon tenders to give an increased range. (Strathwood Library Collection)

Several of the class were to be used as the last regular steam bankers from Tebay to Shap, with which many readers will be familiar, such as No. 75032, lending a helping hand to a goods at Scout Green on 7 October 1967. (Jerry Beddows)

Stopped on the curves at Reading West in 1964 is No. 75066, with a goods for the Southern Region. (Bob Treacher/Alton Model Centre)

Above: Given a repaint into plain unlined black to see out its time was No. 75062, stopped at Derby in January 1967, paired with the BR2A type of tender with 3,500 gallons water capacity. The main advantage of this modified tender was the fall plate to reduce draughts for the crew. (Late Norman Browne/Strathwood Library Collection)

Left: Pushing its BR2 tender with the same 3,500-gallon capacity in reverse is No. 75043 at Arnside in August 1967. (Late Alan Marriottl/ Strathwood Library Collection)

The Southern, as mentioned, preferred the BR1B tender which also afforded an extra ton in coal capacity as No. 75075 demonstrates the need, accelerating through Milbrook in October 1966. (Michael Beaton)

A pleasing elevated view from the road bridge by Holyhead's turntable as a work-stained No. 75054 is pulled around by the fireman in preparation for its onward journey in 1964. (Stewart Blencowe Collection)

Cleaned up for their final duties on enthusiasts' specials are Nos 75019 and 75027, awaiting the guards signal at Carnforth on 28 July 1968 with just hours to go for the last members of this once eighty-strong class. (Strathwood Library Collection)

With a Standard Class 5MT behind we can see the profile of the Southern's style of double chimney fitted to No. 75074 here at Nine Elms on 10 October 1964. (Frank Hornby)

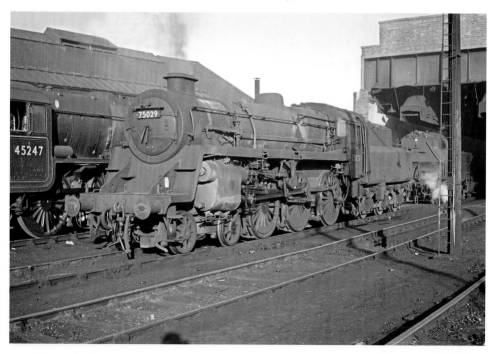

The Western Region had its own design of double chimney fitted to No. 75029, seen here at Llandudno Junction in June 1965. This engine carried all three types of chimney at various times in its career. (Late Norman Browne/Strathwood Library Collection)

Tank Engine Designs Prosper Again

During the war years very little was done to develop tank locomotives. Charles Edward Fairburn had replaced Stanier as CME on the LMS and left his assistant H. G. Ivatt to get along with designing new steam locomotives, as Fairburn was principally an electrical engineer. As a result of a meeting in November 1944, the go-ahead was given for both Ivatt's Class 2 2-6-2T design and the 2-6-0 version as a tender locomotive. The first batches of ten engines of each type were expanded as time went on, from the first built in 1945 until the last entered traffic in 1952. Construction was shared between Crewe with 120 examples and Derby with just 10 locomotives of which No. 41320 seen here at Weymouth on 22 January 1967 was the first from the former Midland Railway workshops. (Strathwood Library Collection)

Above: A Horsham local is at Guildford in August 1964, with No. 41294 in charge. (Late Norman Browne/Strathwood Library Collection)

Left: At Bournemouth shed in 1964, No. 41312 leans on the tool van for a while. (Trans Pennine Publishing)

Again at Bournemouth Nos 41230 and 41320 keep company together in January 1967. (Strathwood Library Collection)

Several of the class were fitted for push-pull workings, such as No. 41286 taking water at Warrington. The first ninety engines built had 17,410-lb tractive effort, whilst the later builds were given slightly larger cylinders and up-rated to 18,510-lb tractive effort. (Trans Pennine Publishing)

Another push-pull-fitted engine was No. 41211, showing the cut-away bunker, which could hold three tons of coal, as here at Bank Hall on 30 July 1966. Senior shed staff were invited by Ivatt to inspect a full-size wooden mock up of the class before construction proper commenced, to correct any details they felt were pertinent. (Win Wall/Strathwood Library Collection)

From the earlier locomotives, push-pull-fitted No. 41215 shows the original design of chimney fitted whilst on shed at Chester Northgate on 30 August 1959. (Frank Hornby)

A new tapered narrow chimney was developed by Swindon Works, firstly for the tender versions of the design with an improved blast pipe, which was later fitted to some of the tank locomotives such as No. 41294, sandwiched between two Standard 4MTs at Eastleigh in September 1965. (Late Norman Browne/Strathwood Library Collection)

Few modifications were made to Ivatt's original design by the team headed by Riddles and E. S. Cox to be included as Standard designs, as construction continued at Crewe in 1953 after the last of the earlier versions had just left the erecting shops. Among the detail improvements were BR clack valves to replace the LMS top feeds and external regulator rodding. The new design gave the same power output as the later Ivatt engines, with a marginal increase in weight. Out of steam at Wellingborough on 18 June 1961 was No. 84008. (Late Vincent Heckford/Strathwood Library Collection)

The brakes are released on board No. 84002 as she leaves Reading bound for Buttigiegs scrapyard in Newport in 1966, after being a 1E Bletchley engine for most of her service years. (Bob Treacher/Alton Model Centre.)

A second batch of engines was authorised to be built at Darlington as part of the 1957 programme of construction. Among these was No. 84028, at Crewe in a plain black livery on 1 November 1964. These later locomotives were sent first to the Southern Region in the main to Kent where within a few years, electrification and line closures made them redundant and a move to London Midland Region allocations followed. This machine would be among the last eleven in service that were all withdrawn in December 1965. (Dave Hill)

It seems a number of the class may never have been photographed in colour due to their short careers and being unglamorous engines not often in steam. Bucking the trend is No. 84006, in steam at Wellingborough on 25 April 1965 in the last few months of a brief and undistinguished career. (Stewart Blencowe Collection)

One last thread of hope for the class came in December 1965 with the consideration of replacing the ageing Adams Class O2 tanks on the Isle of Wight with the survivors. The only one to venture south was No. 84014, seen here at Eastleigh on 19 December 1965 after the authorities had elected to purchase redundant London Transport tube stock and electrify a much-pruned railway on the island. Such a pity, as how many of us would travel to see them today if they had been kept? (Peter Coton)

A visit to Llandudno Junction in 1964 rewards our cameraman with this view of a reasonably clean No. 84009, again sadly out of steam on shed. Check your collections to see if you captured any of the class as we would be pleased to hear from you. (Len Smith)

Continuing our theme of 2-6-2Ts, we move on to the Class 3 Standard tanks with this view of No. 82015 moving on shed at Eastleigh with No. 41305 of the earlier Ivatt design on 26 March 1960. With no readily available boiler to suit from the LMS stable, the Riddles design team turned towards Swindon and the availability of something suitable, such as the type built for their larger Prairie Classes and the 5600 Class of 0-6-2T. The first three were turned out from Swindon Works in April 1952. (Frank Hornby)

It would be August 1955 when the last of this forty-five-strong class would enter service. No. 82029 on shed here at 70B Feltham in September 1965 was ready in time for Christmas 1954. Perhaps more of interest to the modeller as they read this volume will be comparison of the various styles of numbering and livery versions that seem to have been executed by the different workshops responsible for overhauls. (Win Wall/Strathwood Library Collection)

A wet lunchtime at Bath Green Park in May 1963 and all is quiet, aside from No. 82004 blowing off from the safety valves just before departure with a local service. (Trans Pennine Publishing)

Returning to its birthplace for overhaul and release again in a shiny coat of lined green paint after just under five years of use on 18 October 1959 is No. 82030. Re-entering service at 85A Worcester before another six sheds in her last six years of use, was she trouble, perhaps? (Frank Hornby)

Above: The characteristic stains on the water tanks of Nine Elms-allocated examples are born by No. 82019 on its home shed in 1965. (Strathwood Library Collection)

Left: Retaining evidence of an earlier lined green repaint from Swindon still into April 1966 was No. 82003, on a special at Hayfield. (J Davenport/Strathwood Library Collection)

Wearing plain green and a larger later crest is No. 82020 with fellow class member No. 82021 on shed at Willesden during their transfer movement from Wrexham to Nine Elms in April 1965. (Michael Beaton)

With No. 82015 standing behind Standard Class 4MT 80039 at Eastleigh on 26 March 1960, we come to the largest expression of tank locomotives attributed to either Riddles or Ivatt, with 155 being built at Derby, Brighton and Doncaster Works across a five-year construction period for all of the regions. (Frank Hornby)

The reallocations from one region to another were extensive for this class of engines as electrification, diesel railcars and line closures chased them everywhere they went. Many finally found homes on the Southern Region, where three are seen at Redhill, including No. 80033 under repairs, on 29 November 1964. (Peter Coton)

Above: Another day at Bath Green Park station and the much lamented Somerset & Dorset, which saw many Ivatt and Riddles engines tried on the line. One regular at the end was No. 80043, as here in March 1965. (Edward Dorricott)

Left: Percolating away at Eastleigh on 11 September 1965 with an Ivatt is No. 80137. (Late Norman Browne/Strathwood Library Collection)

Some of the Scottish Region engines had a recess built in to accept tablet-catchers, such as No. 80126 at Perth in 1964. (Len Smith)

Famed for their lively acceleration, No. 80041 makes a steamy departure from Evercreech on the Somerset & Dorset route in November 1965. (Ken Pullin)

Acting as a pilot to West Country No. 34024 *Tamar Valley* at the head of a well-loaded 15.50 Weymouth–Waterloo train is No. 80138, with both engines going well on Upwey Bank during 1966. (Strathwood Library Collection)

Enter the Moguls

Staying on the Southern Region, the later preserved Ivatt Class 4MT 2-6-0 No. 43106 has recently been out shopped from Eastleigh Works and rests on the shed on 10 October 1965. As can be seen in this, the last of the Ivatt designs introduced in 1947, they were expected to be able to travel in reverse for some distances with the comfort of the footplate crew being catered for, compared to so many pre-war designs that must have been hellish in the winter months, running tender first. (Strathwood Library Collection)

Clearly H. G. Ivatt was influenced by the experiences of the American S160 2-8-0 design during the war years, as they ran on UK metals before transfer to occupied Europe. Their high running plate and easy access to all running gear for maintenance, with performance and build cost took priority over form. For the post-war period, life for Britain's railways, as in every other walk of life in the country, was very austere as money was very tight and materials had limited availability. Twenty years later, in the height of the swinging sixties, No. 43033 was making swift progress at Lea Road with a Euston–Blackpool train. (Chris Forrest)

Provision within the tender cab has been made for a tablet-catcher on board No. 43001 at Crewe South on 19 March 1967. (John Green)

Some evidence of tender-first running along branch lines such as on the Langholm line at Gilnockie on 25 May 1964. (Late Roy Hamilton)

Ugly to some and functional to fitters, they quickly picked up nicknames such as Doodlebugs and Flying Pigs. This is No. 43007 at Woodford in 1965. (Bob Treacher/Alton Model Centre)

The high running plate made them easily recognisable at a distance. This is No. 43034 at Crewe South in February 1967. (Colin Rodgers/ Strathwood Library Collection)

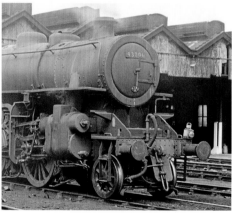

Left: That frontal face looked different somehow when the smoke box number plate was fixed a little higher as on No. 43006 at Barrow in July 1965. (Win Wall/Strathwood Library Collection)

Below: Everything certainly was on show as witnessed on No. 43019 at Lostock Hall on 30 March 1968. (Strathwood Library Collection)

This high running plate theme was perpetuated with the Riddles Standard Class 4MT design, which went into production in 1952 at Doncaster and Horwich almost alongside the last of the Ivatt Class 4 Moguls. Although none of these Standards was built at Darlington unlike the Ivatts, one of the class, No. 76114, would become the very last steam locomotive to be built at Doncaster in 1957. We begin with No. 76098 from a Horwich batch of 1957 seen at Ayr in 1965. (Len Smith)

None were ordered for the Western Region, but all the other regions placed orders, such as the Southern with No. 76067 seen here at Salisbury in 1964, although, as we will see, Swindon did overhaul several. (Trans Pennine Publishing)

Above: Powerful locomotives if required, they were often used on very light turns as well, such as here at Rotherham in 1959 with No. 76056. (Trans Pennine Publishing)

Page opposite above: Also on the Southern and put to use on cross-country services from Reading to Redhill at Ash in October 1964 is No. 76089. (Late Norman Browne/Strathwood Library Collection)

Page opposite below: Popping back out into the sunlight at Bincome Tunnel is No. 76031 on 28 May 1966. (Late Alan Marriott/Strathwood Library Collection)

Below: Shunting stock at Fratton on 14 August 1968, No. 76068 hardly appears taxed either. (Strathwood Library Collection)

Just awaiting the arrival of its tender from overhaul at Swindon Works in March 1964 is No. 76041 and a return to Cricklewood. (Late Norman Browne/Strathwood Library Collection)

Eighteen months later and the future looks grim for No. 76030 along with redundant Maunsell S15s Nos 30833 and 30824 alongside the ferro-concrete shed at Feltham on 5 September 1965. The Mogul has a cab-side provision for fitting a tablet-catcher, certainly now no longer required. (Win Wall/Strathwood Library Collection)

Above: Doncaster-built No. 76067 has the BR1B tender at Salisbury in March 1967. (Strathwood Library Collection)

Below: With the BR2A tender is one of the Horwich engines No. 76088 at Willesden on 8 March 1964. (Frank Hornby)

Fitted with screens is another type BR2A tender, attached to No. 76051 at Harston Sidings on 4 June 1966. The first forty-five engines didn't benefit from the draught protection and were fitted with BR2 tenders when new. (Stewart Blencowe Collection)

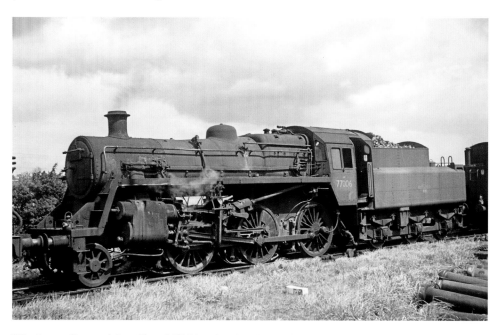

Was there really a need for a Class 3MT Mogul in the scheme of things? With the placing of orders for diesel railcars and diesel locomotives already being considered as the Class 3s came into service from Swindon in 1954, was it really just another job-creation scheme hatched to keep men busy at Swindon Works as the almost endless production of pannier tanks dried up at last? In the lines at Kilmarnock we find No. 77006 between turns in the Ayrshire coalfields in 1965. (Richard Sinclair Collection)

As well as the Scottish Region, the North Eastern Region also took a few engines from the twenty built for use in North Yorkshire and County Durham, such as No. 77012, moving around the shed yard at York in 1962. (John Gill)

Getting away from Beattock is No. 77005, while a perhaps more versatile and useful Black Five remains in the yard. The fitters at Hurlford took great delight in branding the class as Mickey Mouses after finding that Swindon had placed the washout plugs in the wrong places on the boiler, almost resulting in a boiler explosion. The class were taken straight out of use and sent to St Rollox Works for remedial work and Swindon Works was cast into a bad light north of the border. (Trans Pennine Publishing)

Seen again at York in March 1967, but now in plain black, possibly to mask the scrape along the BR2A tender as the type fitted to all of the class. The design was a bit of a disaster really, as various problems came to light in everyday use, such as the fall plate becoming as sharp as a razor from the constant slicing action of engine and tender in use. This movement allowed a lot of coal to be dropped over the side from the footplate out on the road, coupled with the drain holes in the base of the coal space becoming blocked up and at the end of shifts both coal and water being picked up on the fireman's shovel for the fire. This said, the class did have a few admirers. (Colin Rogers/Strathwood Library Collection)

Riddles only tidied up an already successful design from Ivatt with the Standard 2MT Moguls. Standing among more powerful engines at Willesden is No. 78018 on 8 March 1964. (Frank Hornby)

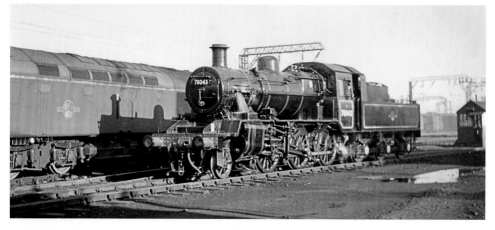

Above: Built at Darlington and now ex-works from Crewe at 5A alongside an English Electric Type 4 in 1961 is No. 78043. (Strathwood Library Collection)

Below: Standing in the cold winter air at Willesden in January 1965, No. 78063 is ready to move off shed. (Strathwood Library Collection)

The similar treatment of the running plate with a front drop panel combined with a more gentle contour to the cab sides resulted in both an attractive and very practical engine, of which sixty-five were ordered and constructed between 1952 and 1956 for all but the Southern Region. Crewe North this time plays host to an ex-works No. 78058 in November 1963. (Richard Sinclair Collection)

Designated as a type BR3 tender and fitted to all of the class, it was very suitable for reverse-running if required, such as here with No. 78054 on a tour train at Edinburgh St Leonards on the BLS/SLS Scottish Rambler No.4 on 19 April 1965. This particular engine had previously enjoyed service on the ex-Great North of Scotland Railway's lines, where its light nature was well suited. (Strathwood Library Collection)

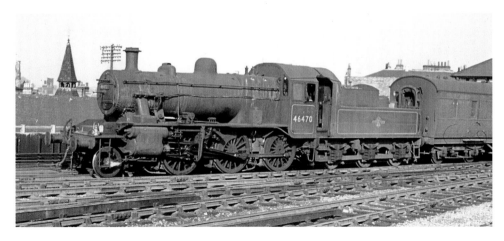

Above: The connection with Swindon also resulted, as previously mentioned, in an improved chimney and blast pipe, although it detracted from looks perhaps on No. 46470 seen at Leamington in 1963. (Tim Meredith)

Page opposite above: The top feed and running plate are what first give away the appearance of the original Ivatt design, as here with No. 46516 with a Carmarthen–Aberystwyth train at Pantybwr in August 1961. (Strathwood Library Collection)

Page opposite below: The flatter nature of the cab on the original Ivatt design is apparent here on No. 46517 at Middlewich whilst on a tour train. As might be expected on Swindon-built engines, this example has found itself painted into an attractive lined green livery. Other engines in the class would be built at Crewe and Darlington, with construction running from 1946 until 1953, by which time the Riddles versions were being built as well. (Trans Pennine Publishing)

Below: Standing next to an impressive ex-Lancashire and Yorkshire Railway water crane at Newton Heath, we find No. 46505 again from Swindon on 22 April 1967. The coal capacity of both the Riddles and the Ivatt tenders was 4 tons. (Michael Beaton)

Another engine turned out in a simple plain unlined black livery was No. 46441, one of four to survive into preservation. However, no thoughts were given towards that when it was seen at Lancaster in 1963. (Len Smith)

This time a plain green livery is worn by No. 46509, penetrating into Southern suburban territory at Teddington on 27 July 1965 with a rail tour. The first of these Ivatts was taken out of service in December 1961 with a real flurry of withdrawals in 1967 to see the class off. (Derek Swetnam)

Perhaps the Best Came Last

Among all of the designs featured in this book, even allowing for the failure of the Crosti 9Fs the class was well regarded by enthusiasts and enginemen alike. Poking out into the sun at Wellingborough shed like a cuckoo on 8 November 1964, Class 9F No. 92112, even filthy dirty, makes an impressive sight. (Strathwood Library Collection)

At least two gentlemen on the seawall at Dawlish stop for a moment to watch the passing of No. 92207 in June 1959, which was its first month in service. (Alan Pike OBE)

Only sheep and our anonymous cameraman are on hand to watch the passage of No. 92161 along the Settle and Carlisle line at Ais Gill in 1965. (Strathwood Library Collection)

Looking as though she would be much loved again in the future at Chester is No. 92203 in March 1967. (Dave Livesey)

Above: Just another beast of burden to the men of Kingmoor was No. 92116 on 26 August 1966. (Strathwood Library Collection)

Below: At Farrington Junction in 1967, No. 92017 just gets on with the task at hand, with very little fuss. (Michael Beaton)

Steam to spare for No. 92004 with a fitted freight at Newton le Willows on the up line on 17 June 1967. The experience gained by Riddles of the Austerity 2-10-0s during the war years, kept leading the team back to this wheel arrangement from the proposals of 2-8-2s. At a time when almost all freight still travelled by rail it seemed sensible to develop this arrangement, although the Modernisation Plan was just around the corner with waves of orders for diesels and electric traction to follow. (Jerry Beddows)

For many 9Fs on similar duties just after introduction and only a dozen or so years of useful life when perhaps many more could have been made, and just maybe the justification for retaining a British coal industry to support their use into the seventies and eighties. Although in this carbon conscious age in which we now live very few greenies would have much time for 9Fs, such as No. 92204, almost new when seen in June 1959 at Exeter St. Davids. (Alan Pike OBE)

Ramping at the safety valves and with the injectors on to satisfy an efficient boiler on No. 92114 with a lightweight train of empties at Lostock Hall in 1967. Today the same empty load would consume how much imported diesel? (Len Smith)

The safety valves again lift on an impatient No. 92208, given the starter at Tebay to move forward to take on a banker for the climb ahead. Production was shared between Crewe and Swindon across six years as they built the fleet of 251 engines. (Strathwood Library Collection)

Two main types of chimney were used for the production engines. Firstly a single chimney as on the nearest locomotive, then the double blast pipe and chimney fitted to later examples on the rear 9F. (Michael Beaton)

The Giesl oblong ejector was fitted to a number of engines in a bid to improve coal consumption, including a Bulleid Pacific No. 34064 *Fighter Command*, several Riddles Austerity designs in industrial use and to one 9F, also the last steam locomotive built at Crewe, No. 92250, which would also be the highest number in the regular numbering of British Railways locomotives. Very little improvement was noticeable and the 9F worked mostly around South Wales while in service, making a visit to Severn Tunnel Junction shed here on 12 July 1964. (Strathwood Library Collection)

Further experimentation was carried out previously to utilise the Crosti pre-heating system with ten engines from the production run at Crewe being so fitted in 1955. Apparently there were originally to have been fifteen built, all for the Western Region. Among these was No. 92022, like all its nine sisters, which went to Wellingborough in the end. Of these, No. 92022 was in store for three years of its twelve-year service record, as here in June 1961, over a year after *Evening Star* entered traffic. (Late Vincent Heckford/Strathwood Library Collection)

Above: The rebuilt engines such as No. 92026, seen on Birkenhead, were classified as 8F after conversion back to conventionally steamed locomotives. (Stewart Blencowe Collection)

Below: Looking more like an American S160 from this angle, a rebuilt No. 92025 is on Carnforth shed on 7 October 1967, attempting to pay back the wasted investment in the Crosti system. (John Green)

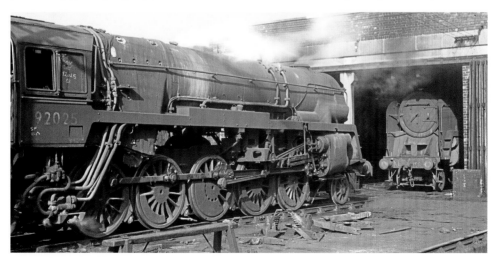

Tender designs varied among the class, such as No. 92204, seen at Carlisle, this time on the avoiding lines with the BR1G tender which afforded 5,000-gallons of water and 7 tons of coal as fitted on 14 October 1967. (Strathwood Library Collection)

An alternative was available in the form of a BR1C tender, mated to No. 92135 running light engine on the down line at Garsdale on 5 July 1967, which gave 250 gallons less water but increased coal capacity to 9 tons. (Jerry Beddows)

To deal with an increased need for boiler water on routes perhaps less afforded by the provisions of water troughs, a BR1F tender was available, bringing a huge (by British standards) 5,625-gallon water capacity along with up to 7 tons of coal. The weight of such a tender in full working order would be 7 tons more than one of Riddles J94 Austerity 0-6-0ST locomotives! Ready for the road at New England is No. 92183 on 10 April 1960. (Frank Hornby)

Three locomotives No. 92165 to No. 92167 would be tested with Berkeley mechanical stokers in an attempt to reach a higher degree of efficiency than that attainable with one fireman. To accommodate this apparatus in the BR1K tender, the water capacity had to be reduced to 4,325 gallons. Although the system was aborted, this engine No. 92167 would become one of the last three 9Fs when withdrawn in July 1968. (Chris Forrest)

A further variety within the class was fitted to the perhaps hardest-worked of all of the locomotives covered in this book, namely the 9Fs, equipped for working the heavy iron ore trains from Tyne Dock to Consett, which is a hilly route to say the least. These engines were specially fitted with air pumps to operate the hoppers on the wagons dedicated to these trains. Ten locomotives were fitted for the arduous duties and paired to BR1B tenders to suit. Taking a rest from these turns on York shed in 1964 is No. 92061. (Douglas Paul)

With another 9F in the rear, No. 92063 digs into the climb at Pelaw in 1965. This same engine had the honour of hauling the last steam-operated train on these services on 19 November 1966, after which the duty was handed over to pairs of specially adapted Sulzer Class 24s. (Noel Marrison)

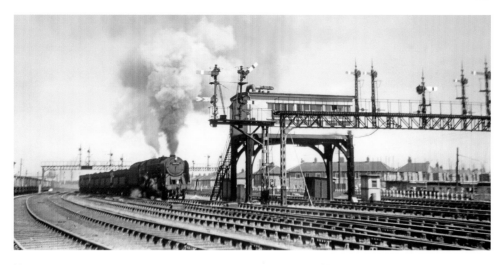

The climb from sea level started straightaway from the dockside past Tyne Dock shed and under the superb North Eastern Railway overhead signal box and large signal gantry as here with No. 92098, blowing off yet still being worked hard. Full credit to engine crews familiar with the line. (Dave Hill)

Between ships arriving from Sweden, either the engines would rest up as here on Tyne Dock shed with Nos 92065 and 92066, on 28 September 1963 or they would be found turns on local coal traffic, which were usually available to the shed foreman if required. (Strathwood Library Collection)

Some legendary passenger workings have been undertaken by 9Fs, not just on the Somerset & Dorset at the hands of Peter Smith and Donald Beale, but also during summer months when the likes of 9Fs were pressed into use for extras or in the event of failures of the rostered engines. The East Coast Main Line near Retford shows a double peg to No. 92172 as it rushes a rake of Mark 1 coaches along in 1961. (Trans Pennine Publishing)

One such summer Saturday extra is hustled along in brisk fashion through Dore and Totley in 1959 by No. 92117. (Trans Pennine Publishing)

Some would say that the connivance of the management at Swindon taking their time over the construction of these superb Riddles 2-10-0s to ensure that Crewe had despatched the last of their orders with the release of No. 92250 to traffic in December 1958 allowed Swindon the luxury of being the locomotive works with the honour of building the very last steam locomotive for British Railways in March 1960. This was No. 92220, named *Evening Star* in a traditional Great Western style and adorned with a lined green livery, and of course the notoriety of the *Rocket* some 135 years before when it all started. (Strathwood Library Collection)

A trifle over optimistic perhaps for No. 92220 *Evening Star*, heading the SCTS special Farewell to Steam Tour of 20 September 1964, seen here at Alton. In fact it would be almost another four years before engines designed by Stanier and one from Robin Riddles, namely No. 70013 *Oliver Cromwell* would have the real honour of the last steam special on the main line for British Railways in August 1968. A few final titbits of Standards trivia perhaps: the only year that all 251 9Fs were available for traffic for a full year was coincidently the only time all 999 British Railways Standards were on the books all together at once for just one month, this was when the last Crosti rebuild No. 92026 came back into traffic and the first Standard, a Class 4MT No. 80103 was withdrawn due to a twisted frame in July of 1962. (Strathwood Library Collection)